Michael M. Dediu

World Opportunities for All

Moving from few local jobs, to world opportunities for all

DERC Publishing House
Nashua, New Hampshire, U. S. A.

Published and printed in the
United States of America
On the Great Seal of the United States are included:
E Pluribus Unum (Out of many, one)
Annuit Coeptis (He has approved of the undertakings)
Novus Ordo Seclorum (New order of the ages)

Library of Congress Control Number: 2020924389

Dediu, Michael M.

World Opportunities for All
Moving from few local jobs, to world opportunities for all

ISBN-13: 978-1-950999-26-2

Preface

Primum vivere, deinde philosophari – first live, then do philosophy. With a new and good Constitution of the World, we can concentrate to live better, to have plenty of opportunities and jobs, moving from few local jobs, to world opportunities for all. Imagine what an improvement in the life of all people!

There are millions of great world opportunities – we give just over 70 examples, from Establishing a permanent peace and Transforming cities in capitals, to Maintenance of the World Government and Increasing global wealth.

From the great philosophers Socrates, Plato, Aristotle, Descartes, and Kant, to the present day, many people dreamed of having really big and useful opportunities all over the world – finally, now we will have them, for the benefit of all people.

This book discusses over 70 opportunities, giving some details, emphasizing that these opportunities and the new ideas from the Constitution of the World, will create the conditions for a peaceful, free and prosperous new country for all - Peaceful Terra.

The future begins to take shape in front of our eyes, and it is incredibly attractive!

Michael M. Dediu, Ph. D.

Nashua, New Hampshire, U. S. A., 8 December 2020

USA, Chicago (1833): Fourth Presbyterian Church (right center, 1871), Elysées Condominiums (center-right, 1972, 56 floors, 161 m), Loyola University of Chicago (red center down, 1870, 1927 this building), Park Tower (center-left, 2000, 67 floors, 257 m).

Table of Contents

Italy, Rome (753 BC, one of the oldest continuously occupied cities in Europe, called Roma Aeterna (The Eternal City) and Caput Mundi (Capital of the World)), in Villa Borghese (1630), a monument (1905, by Lucien Pallez, donated by the French Government) to Victor Hugo (1802 – 1885, the greatest French writer (Hernani (1830, inspired opera Ernani (1844) by Giuseppe Verdi (1813-1901)), Notre-Dame de Paris (1831), Le roi s'amuse (1832, inspired opera Rigoletto (1851) by Giuseppe Verdi)), Les Misérables (1862), Les Contemplations, La Légendre des siècles)).

Opportunity 1. No more war

Description: This opportunity is simply to work for the elimination of war and any type of conflicts on Earth, making possible for all the people on Earth to live better, peacefully, free, healthy, and prosperous.

Qualifications: All people can apply.

Starting day: 1 January 2021

Ending day: continuous

Salary: From the minimum wage to over $100,000/year

Possibility of promotion or transfer to another job: Yes, for good performers.

Comments: It is a matter of common sense – all people want peace, freedom, good health, harmony and prosperity.
For all the opportunities, people will work in well-organized organizations, with a very clear and urgent objectives.

USA, the University of California, Berkeley (1868, named after the philosopher and mathematician Bishop George Berkeley (1685-1753), motto Fiat lux (Let there be light), 36,200 students, major public research university, 72 Nobel laureates, between the top six universities in the world, 500 ha campus), il Campanile (Sather Tower (61 bells (full concert carillon) and clock tower). 1914, 94 m, 7 floors, observation deck on the 8th floor, inspired by il Campanile (850, 1514, 1912, 99 m) di San Marco (1084), Venezia (421, Venice), Italy (900 BC)).

Opportunity 2. Establishing a permanent peace

Description: The objective of this opportunity is to have a lasting peace, without any conflicts on Earth, making possible for all the people on Earth to live better, peacefully, free, healthy, and prosperous.

Qualifications: All people can apply.

Starting day: 1 January 2021

Ending day: continuous

Salary: From $20,000/year.

Possibility of promotion or transfer to another job: Yes, for good performers.

Comments: It is a matter of common sense – all people want peace, freedom, good health, harmony and prosperity.

It is not sufficient to just eliminate war - we need to build a very strong and long-lasting Peace, because without peace not much else can be done. People want a Peaceful Terra.

Opportunity 3. Taking care of 509 M km^2 of land and water

Description: The objective of this Opportunity is to properly manage all the planet for all people.

Qualifications: People with knowledge and experience in this area.

Starting day: 1 January 2021

Ending day: continuous work.

Salary: From $20,000year.

Possibility of promotion or transfer to another job: Yes.

Comments: The people will always have priority, with a proper balance. People will work for self-supporting institutions, which focus on clean and beautiful Earth for all people.

Opportunity 4. Less bureaucratic rules

Description: The objective of this opportunity is simply to eliminate the many superfluous rules, which create bureaucracy.

Qualifications: People with knowledge and experience in this area.

Starting day: 1 January 2021

Ending day: continuous

Salary: From $20,000/year

Possibility of promotion or transfer to another job: Yes.

Comments: This will be a continuous effort by all people - those who get excellent results will be compensated.

UK, London, from a bus on Queen Victoria St, looking west to St Mary Aldemary (a church has been at this site for over 900 years, from around 1100, then rebuilding and restorations took place in 1510, 1629, 1704, 1877, 2005; it is an Anglican church in Bow Lane). In 1781 a new organ was installed, built by George England (1740-1788) and Hugh Russell. The church as rebuilt has an aisled nave, six bays long, with a clerestory.

Opportunity 5. Create 10 friendly regions

Description: The objective of this opportunity is to create the conditions for a good and efficient management of the country Peaceful Terra.

Qualifications: People with knowledge and experience in this area.

Starting day: 1 January 2021

Ending day: 6 months after the starting day.

Salary: From $48,000

Possibility of promotion or transfer to another job: Yes.

Comments: All people will participate. For easier administration, Peaceful Terra will be only administratively divided in 10 simple and friendly regions of around 770 M people each, called R0, R1,…, R9, which will be delimited by meridians (or line of longitudes), with the assistance of the United Nations.

Opportunity 6. Transform cities in capitals

Description: The objective of this opportunity is to begin work for the preparation of many cities, which will become capitals.

Qualifications: People with knowledge and experience in this area.

Starting day: 1 January 2021

Ending day: 6 months after the starting day.

Salary: From $32,000/year

Possibility of promotion or transfer to another job: Yes.

Comments: Capitals will be everywhere, because the current capitals tend to become huge bureaucracies, with lots of people trying to be there, without much usefulness. Peaceful Terra will have moving capitals, to benefit everybody.

Each region will have a pair of capitals plus an outside city, for better and more homogenous management. (all will change every year; more details are in the book "World with One Country & its Ten Friendly Regions - Moving from 195 disagreeing countries, to 1 country with 10 collaborating regions"). For example, the first implementation will be:

R0 between meridians 0 and 15^0 E, capitals: Bern (Switzerland), Libreville (Gabon), and Oxford (UK).

R1: 15^0 E - 30^0 E, Warsaw (Poland), Pretoria (South Africa) and Miami (FL, USA).

R2: 30^0 E - 45^0 E, Moscow (Russia), Cairo (Egypt), and Grenoble (France).

R3: 45^0 E - 75^0 E, Astana (Kazakhstan), Karachi (Pakistan), and Montpellier (France).

R4: 75^0 E - 85^0 E, New Delhi (India), Novosibirsk (Russia), and Magdeburg (Germany).

R5: 85^0 E - 100^0 E, Krasnoyarsk (Russia), Urumqi (China), and Avignon (France).
R6: 100^0 E - 115^0 E, Jakarta (Indonesia), Beijing (China), and Neuchâtel (Switzerland).
R7: 115^0 E - 180^0, Tokyo (Japan), Sydney (Australia), and Malmö (Sweden).
R8: 180^0 - 70^0 Washington (USA), Mexico City (Mexico), and Bellinzona (Switzerland).
R9: 70^0 W – 0 Halifax (Canada), Brasilia (Brazil), and Biel (Switzerland).

There are many big differences between the number of people in different regions, in the first implementation, and then between the populations of different sub-regions, but this is just the first implementation, which needs to be quickly put in place, and then, very easily, the delimitations will be moved a few kilometers east or west, to reach a balanced population (same number of people).

Because all the people are in the same country, it is normal to modify a little its regions, for better administration, to make everybody happy.

It is well understood that there will be some difficulties in the beginning, like in all beginnings, but with calm, patience, perseverance and hard work, the things will improve fast, and all the people will enjoy a better life.

The city Niagara Falls, Ontario, Canada, with its Skylon Tower (center-left, 1965, 160 m, a Revolving Dining Room), and the boarding place (center-right) for the boat to the Horseshoe Falls.

Switzerland, Geneva, the Monument (1879) for Charles II, Duke of Brunswick (30 Oct 1804 in Brunswick (Braunschweig), Germany-19 August 1873, aged 68.8 (died in Geneva at Beau Rivage Hotel), ruled the Duchy of Brunswick 1815-1830).

Opportunity 7. Work on sub-regions and districts

Description: The objective of this opportunity is to define the sub-regions and districts, for better administration of the help for people.

Qualifications: People with knowledge and experience in this area.

Starting day: 1 July 2021

Ending day: 6 months after the starting day.

Salary: From $29,000/year

Possibility of promotion or transfer to another job: Yes.

Comments: Each of the 10 regions will be divided by meridians in 10 sub-regions S00, , S99, each with about 77 M people.

Then each of the 100 sub-regions will be divided in 10 districts: D000, D001, , D999, each with about 7.7 M people, and each of the districts will have their current small and big cities.

All these delimitations between regions, as well as between sub-regions, will be flexible: these will be just simple administrative delimitations – they will be changed after each census (5 years), for maintaining a balanced number of people in all regions (around 770 M) and sub-regions (around 77 M).

Opportunity 8. Help to have telework for all

Description: The objective of this opportunity is to extend and improve telework for all.

Qualifications: People with knowledge and experience in this area.

Starting day: 1 January 2021

Ending day: continuous

Salary: From $28,000/year

Possibility of promotion or transfer to another job: Yes.

Comments: This is the future – with telework many people will have a northern residence and a southern residence, seasonally moving from one to the other, to avoid extreme cold or heat, and having the same hour.

.

Opportunity 9. Enjoyable oceans for all

Description: The objective of this opportunity is to carefully manage all the oceans for all the people.

Qualifications: People with knowledge and experience in this area.

Starting day: 1 January 2021

Ending day: continuous

Salary: From $35,000/year

Possibility of promotion or transfer to another job: Yes.

Comments: The oceans are important for people and for our planet. All the oceans will belong to some of the regions, therefore will be maintained by those regions, to be free of any piracy or other bad activity – World Police will help when necessary.

France, Paris, Tour Eiffel (1889, 324 m, 279 m at the 3rd level, looking north-west): Tour Eiffel shadow (center), Pont d'Iéna over La Seine (left down), Avenue de New York (green, on the north side of La Seine), Jardin du Trocadéro (1878, 1937, with the Fountain of Warsaw (center left)), Palais de Chaillot (center up), Port de Suffren (down left), Port de la Bourdonnais (down right), Ave. d'Eylau (up-left, vertical), Av. Albert de Mun (center right).

Opportunity 10. Explain the World Government

Description: The objective of this opportunity is to keep people correctly informed about the World Government, in order to improve it.

Qualifications: People with knowledge and experience in this area.

Starting day: 1 January 2021

Ending day: continuous

Salary: From $25,000/year

Possibility of promotion or transfer to another job: Yes.

Comments: It is important for people to know the World Government, in order to have peace, freedom, good health, harmony and prosperity. Peaceful Terra, with its family of over 7.7 B people, will have four levels of world management: at the local level, if needed, it could be one or two more levels of local managers (mayors, town managers, county managers – all levels of management must be friendly, helpful, fast, polite, modest and smart):

Level 1 Managers: 1,000 L1 friendly managers, for the 1,000 districts, who will supervise and assist the mayors and town managers from their district, for a total of about 7,700,000 people in each district. Each of the 1,000 L1 friendly managers will be located in a central city from their districts – they could be the mayors of those cities, but with new responsibilities for the whole district.

Level 2 Qualifications: 100 L2 friendly managers, for the 100 sub-regions, who will supervise and assist the 10 L1 managers of the 10 districts of each sub-region, for a total of about 77,000,000 people for each sub-region. These 100 L2 friendly managers will move each month between the two capitals of each of the 100 sub-regions.

Level 3 Managers: 10 L3 friendly managers for the 10 regions.

Level 4 Managers: 10 L4 friendly advisers for the world.

UK, Oxford, a Public Library close to Christ Church College (1546) and Merton College (1264, named after Walter de Merton).

France, Paris - The central part of the façade of L'Opéra de Paris (1875): composers Daniel Auber (1782–1871, left), Ludwig van Beethoven (1770–1827, second), Wolfgang Amadeus Mozart (1756–1791, center) and Gaspare Spontini (1774–1851, right).

UK, London, from Parliament Square, looking southwest to the Church of St Margaret of Antioch (1523, the Anglican parish church of the House of Commons), 20 m northeast of the Westminster Abbey.

Opportunity 11. Work on the two capitals for each sub-region

Description: The objective of this opportunity is to prepare 200 cities to be sub-region capitals.

Qualifications: People with knowledge and experience in this area.

Starting day: 1 March 2021

Ending day: 6 months after the starting day

Salary: From 36,000/year

Possibility of promotion or transfer to another job: Yes.

Comments: It is relevant to have many cities refreshed and prepared to be capitals of sub-regions.

For example: in the beginning these capitals will be:

In Region R0: from Paris (France) to N'Djamena (Chad)

- The sub-region R00 will have the capitals Paris (France) and Niamey (Niger) – assistance from Magdeburg (Germany).
- The sub-region R01 will have the capitals Brussels (Belgium) and Porto-Novo (Benin) - assistance from Toronto (Canada).
- The sub-region R02 will have the capitals Amsterdam (Netherlands) and Algiers (Algeria) - assistance from Graz (Austria).
- The sub-region R03 will have the capitals Luxembourg (Luxembourg) and Sao Tome (Sao Tome and Principe) - assistance from Adelaide (Australia).
- The sub-region R04 will have the capitals of Abuja (Nigeria) and Bochum (Germany) - assistance from Nikko (Japan).

- The sub-region R05 will have the capitals Malabo (Equatorial Guinea), and Zürich (Switzerland) - assistance from Leeds (UK).
- The sub-region R06 will have the capitals Oslo (Norway) and Tunis (Tunisia) - assistance from Sheffield (UK).
- The sub-region R07 will have the capitals Roma (Italy) and Luanda (Angola) - assistance from Yamagata (Japan).
- The sub-region R08 will have the capitals in Berlin (Germany) and Tripoli (Libya) - assistance from New York (USA).
- The sub-region R09 will have the capitals Prague (Czech Republic) and N'Djamena (Chad) - assistance from Brisbane (Australia).

Italy, Rome: The east side of the Mausoleum (135-139) of Hadrian (76–138, Emperor 117-138, renamed Castel Sant'Angelo in 600). It was used by the popes as a castle and now is a museum.

USA, Chicago (1833): Chicago Water Works (down, 1869, was pumping station, survived fire in 1871, now base for the Lookingglass Theatre Company), Water Tower Place (right, 1976, 74 fl, 261 m), John Hancock Center (left up, 1969, 100 fl, 457 m with antenna).

UK, Cambridge, a bas-relief on the eastern wall of the western building of the Old Court (1451) of Queens' College (1448).

In Region R1: from Zagreb (Croatia) to Bujumbura (Burundi)

- The sub-region R10 will have the capitals in Zagreb (Croatia) and Brazzaville (Congo) - assistance from Nantes (France).
- The sub-region R11 will have the capitals in Vienna (Austria), Windhoek (Namibia) - assistance from Bilbao (Spain).
- The sub-region R12 will have the capitals in Stockholm (Sweden), Bangui (Central African Republic) - assistance from Florence (Italy).
- The sub-region R13 will have the capitals in Budapest (Hungary), Rundu (Namibia) - assistance from Monaco (Monaco).
- The sub-region R14 will have the capitals in Belgrade (Serbia), Kananga (Democratic Republic of Congo) - assistance from Liverpool (UK).
- The sub-region R15 will have the capitals in Athens (Greece), Mongu (Zambia) - assistance from Los Angeles (CA, USA).
- The sub-region R16 will have the capitals in Helsinki (Finland) and Kolwezi (Democratic Republic of the Congo) - assistance from Montreal (Canada).
- The sub-region R17 will have the capitals in Bucharest (Romania) and Gaborone (Botswana) - assistance from Philadelphia (PA, USA).
- The sub-region R18 will have the capitals in Minsk (Belarus) and Maseru (Lesotho) - assistance from Orleans (France).
- The sub-region R19 will have the capitals in Chisinau (Republic of Moldova) and Bujumbura (Burundi) - assistance from Hamburg (Germany).

Constanta, Romania, Piazza Ovidiu: Statue of Publius Ovidius Naso (20 March 43 BC, in Sulmona – 17, in Tomis, Moesia (now Constanta, Romania), aged circa 59, close to the place where Ovidius died.

In Region R2: from Kiev (Ukraine) to Baghdad (Iraq)

- The sub-region R20 will have the capitals in Kiev (Ukraine) and Kigali (Rwanda) - assistance from Ottawa (Canada).
- The sub-region R21 will have the capitals in Ankara (Turkey) and Khartoum (Sudan) - assistance from Salzburg (Austria).
- The sub-region R22 will have the capitals in Lilongwe (Malawi) and Nicosia (Cyprus) - assistance from Dallas (TX, USA).
- The sub-region R23 will have the capitals in Jerusalem (Israel) and Dodoma (Tanzania) - assistance from Strasbourg (France).
- The sub-region R24 will have the capitals in Damascus (Syria) and Nairobi (Kenya) - assistance from Stuttgart (Germany).
- The sub-region R25 will have the capitals in Krasnodar (Russia) and Addis Ababa (Ethiopia) - assistance from Marseille (France).
- The sub-region R26 will have the capitals in Rostov-on-Don (Russia) and Asmara (Eritrea) - assistance from Leipzig (Germany).
- The sub-region R27 will have the capitals in Stavropol (Russia) and Djibouti (Djibouti) - assistance from Zürich (Switzerland).
- The sub-region R28 will have the capitals in Mosul (Iraq) and Moroni (Comoros) - assistance from Linz (Austria).
- The sub-region R29 will have the capitals in Yerevan (Armenia) and Baghdad (Iraq) - assistance from Göttingen (Germany).

London: From the Westminster Bridge (1862) looking southwest to the Palace of Westminster (1016, 1870), Big Ben (1855, 96 m, right).

Germany - 23 March 1978, Freibourg im Breisgau (1120 by Duke Berthold III of Zähringen (1085-1122), elevation 278 m, the south façade of Freiburger Münster (cathedral, 1200, 116 m, J. S. Bach (1685-1750) performed here).

In Region R3: from Riyadh (Saudi Arabia) to Malé (Maldives)

- The sub-region R30 will have the capitals in Riyadh (Saudi Arabia) and Mogadishu (Somalia) - assistance from Bonn (Germany).
- The sub-region R31 will have the capitals in Baku (Azerbaijan) and Antananarivo (Madagascar) - assistance from Le Mans (France).
- The sub-region R32 will have the capitals in Oral (Kazakhstan) and Tehran (Iran) - assistance from Pisa (Italy).
- The sub-region R33 will have the capitals in Ashgabat (Turkmenistan) and Abu Dhabi (United Arab Emirates) - assistance from Wolfsburg (Germany).
- The sub-region R34 will have the capitals in Magnitogorsk (Russia) and Muscat (Oman) - assistance from Toulouse (France).
- The sub-region R35 will have the capitals in Chelyabinsk (Russia) and Herat (Afghanistan) - assistance from Basel (Switzerland).
- The sub-region R36 will have the capitals in Tyumen (Russia) and Kandahar (Afghanistan) - assistance from Nagoya (Japan).
- The sub-region R37 will have the capitals in Dushanbe (Tajikistan) and Labytnangi (Russia) - assistance from Limoges (France).
- The sub-region R38 will have the capitals in Tashkent (Uzbekistan) and Kabul (Afghanistan) - assistance from Rostock (Germany).
- The sub-region R39 will have the capitals in Islamabad (Pakistan) and Malé (Maldives) - assistance from La Rochelle (France).

Japan, Osaka (645 AD, the 3rd largest city in Japan, capital of Osaka Prefecture on the main island Honshu): detail of Toyosaki shrine (1772, with the Emperor Kotoku and others enshrined here).

Italy, Rome: Accademia Nazionale dei Lincei (1603) in Villa Farnesina (1510). The author was invited to give a lecture here in 1978.

In Region R4: from Bishkek (Kyrgyzstan) to Brahmapur (India)

- The sub-region R40 will have the capitals in Bishkek (Kyrgyzstan) and Jaipur (India) - assistance from Osaka (Japan).
- The sub-region R41 will have the capitals in Akola (India) and Kashgar (China) - assistance from Genoa (Italy).
- The sub-region R42 will have the capitals in Almaty (Kazakhstan) and Coimbatore (India) - assistance from Perth (Australia).
- The sub-region R43 will have the capitals in Kuybyshev (Russia) and Agra (India) - assistance from Fukuoka (Japan).
- The sub-region R44 will have the capitals in Vertikos (Russia) and Nagpur (India) - assistance from Coral Bay (Australia).
- The sub-region R45 will have the capitals in Chennai (India) and Colombo (Sri Lanka) - assistance from Sapporo (Japan).
- The sub-region R46 will have the capitals in Lucknow (India) and Fedosikha (Russia) - assistance from Niigata (Japan).
- The sub-region R47 will have the capitals in Bilaspur (India) and Kolpashevo (Russia) - assistance from Albany (Australia).
- The sub-region R48 will have the capitals in Visakhapatnam (India) and Barnaul (Russia) - assistance from Hiroshima (Japan).
- The sub-region R49 will have the capitals in Brahmapur (India) and Tomsk (Russia) - assistance from Yokohama (Japan).

Italy, Rome (753 BC), Vatican (1929): Piazza di San Pietro (1656 – 1667, Bernini), with Moderno's façade (115 m wide, 46 m high) of the Basilica di San Pietro (1506 – 1626), and an Egyptian obelisk.

UK, Oxford, University of Oxford, School of Anthropology and Museum Ethnography, Institute of Social and Cultural Anthropology, at 51 - 53 Banbury Road.

In Region R5: from Kathmandu (Nepal) to Dehong (China)

- The sub-region R50 will have the capitals in Kathmandu (Nepal) and Patna (India) - assistance from Kobe (Japan).
- The sub-region R51 will have the capitals in Bayingol (China) and Novokuznetsk (Russia) - assistance from Vichy (France).
- The sub-region R52 will have the capitals in Thimphu (Bhutan) and Dhaka (Bangladesh) - assistance from Jena (Germany).
- The sub-region R53 will have the capitals in Lhasa (China) and Achinsk (Russia) - assistance from Reims (France).
- The sub-region R54 will have the capitals in Abakan (Russia) and Kumul (China) - assistance from Fribourg (Switzerland).
- The sub-region R55 will have the capitals in Kyzyl (Russia) and Dibrugarh (India) - assistance from Denmark (Australia).
- The sub-region R56 will have the capitals in Bassein (Myanmar) and Tinsukia (India) - assistance from Chiba (Japan).
- The sub-region R57 will have the capitals in Yushu City (China) and Tinskoy (Russia) - assistance from Klagenfurt (Austria).
- The sub-region R58 will have the capitals in Jiuquan (China) and Medan (Indonesia) - assistance from Lucerne (Switzerland).
- The sub-region R59 will have the capitals in Chiang Mai (Thailand) and Dehong (China) - assistance from Mulhouse (France).

Japan, Tokyo (1180), special ward Shinjuku, from the 45th fl., 202 m, of Tokyo Met. Gov Bldg. North Tower): Shinjuku Sumitomo Bldg. (210 m, 52 fl, 1974, center), Shinjuku Mitsui Building (224 m, 55 floors, 1974, right).

In Region R6: from Bangkok (Thailand) to Chita (Russia)

- The sub-region R60 will have the capitals in Bangkok (Thailand) and Kuala Lumpur (Malaysia) - assistance from Besançon (France).
- The sub-region R61 will have the capitals in Vientiane (Laos) and Singapore – assistance from Freiburg im Breisgau (Germany).
- The sub-region R62 will have the capitals in Phnom Penh (Cambodia) and Irkutsk (Russia) – assistance from Baden (Switzerland).
- The sub-region R63 will have the capitals in Palembang (Indonesia), Hanoi (Vietnam) – assistance from Thun (Switzerland).
- The sub-region R64 will have the capitals in Ulan Bator (Mongolia) and Ulan-Ude (Russia) – assistance from Chaumont (France).
- The sub-region R65 will have the capitals in Cirebon (Indonesia) and Nanning (China) – assistance from Vaduz (Lichtenstein).
- The sub-region R66 will have the capitals in Pontianak (Indonesia) and Baotou (China) – assistance from Lugano (Switzerland).
- The sub-region R67 will have the capitals in Surakarta (Indonesia) and Yichang (China) – assistance from Thonon-les-Bain (France).
- The sub-region R68 will have the capitals in Surabaya (Indonesia) and Changsha (China) – assistance from Burgdorf (Switzerland).
- The sub-region R69 will have the capitals in Chita (Russia) and Hong Kong (China) – assistance from Colmar (France).

Venezia: Libreria (left), San Theodore Column, Palazzo Ducale, Lion of Venice Column (center) on Riva degli Schiavoni street.

USA, Boston: a view of the north-east part of Boston, from Cambridge, over Charles River Basin. Federal Reserve Bank Building (187 m, left), and other tall buildings in the financial district.

In Region R7: from Nanchang (China) to Melbourne (Australia)

- The sub-region R70 will have the capitals in Bandar Seri Begawan (Brunei Darussalam) and Nanchang (China) – assistance from Turku (Finland).
- The sub-region R71 will have the capitals in Krasnokamensk (Russia) and Jinan (China) – assistance from St. Gallen (Switzerland).
- The sub-region R72 will have the capitals in Baguio City (Philippines) and Hangzhou (China) – assistance from Dole (France).
- The sub-region R73 will have the capitals in Manila (Philippines) and Taipei (Taiwan, China) – assistance from Metz (France).
- The sub-region R74 will have the capitals in Kupang (Indonesia) and Shanghai (China) – assistance from Davos (Switzerland).
- The sub-region R75 will have the capitals in Pyongyang (North Korea) and Seoul (South Korea) – assistance from Versailles (France).
- The sub-region R76 will have the capitals in Vladivostok (Russia) and Busan (South Korea) – assistance from Innsbruck (Austria).
- The sub-region R77 will have the capitals in Kyoto (Japan) and Khabarovsk (Russia) – assistance from Germering (Germany).
- The sub-region R78 will have the capitals in Nagoya (Japan) and Komsomolsk-on-Amur (Russia) – assistance from Venice (Italy).
- The sub-region R79 will have the capitals in Sendai (Japan) and Melbourne (Australia) – assistance from St. Moritz (Switzerland).

USA, Niagara Falls (8000 BC, the highest flow rate in the world), with the American Falls (left, USA, 21-30 m drop, 290 m wide), the Bridal Veil Falls (center, USA, 21 m drop, 10 m wide) and the Horseshoe Falls (center-right, in Canada, 53 m drop, 790 m wide).

USA, Chicago (1833): above entrance decorations of the Tribune Tower (1925, 36 floors, 141 m, for Chicago Tribune (1847)), with stones from famous places around the world, and from the Moon, including Harvard University, Arc de Triomph, Switzerland, Great Wall, Parthenon, Taj Mahal, Notre-Dame, and St. Peter's Basilica.

In Region R8: from Anchorage (Alaska, USA) to Lima (Peru)

- The sub-region R80 will have the capitals in Uelen (Russia) and Anchorage (Alaska, USA), – assistance from Zug (Switzerland).
- The sub-region R81 will have the capitals in Vancouver (Canada) and San Jose (CA, USA) – assistance from Odense (Denmark).
- The sub-region R82 will have the capitals in Vernon (Canada) and Los Angeles (CA, USA) – assistance from Amstetten (Austria).
- The sub-region R83 will have the capitals in Calgary (Canada) and Tijuana (Mexico) – assistance from Chur (Switzerland).
- The sub-region R84 will have the capitals in Hermosillo (Mexico) and Tucson (AR, USA) – assistance from Bergen (Norway).
- The sub-region R85 will have the capitals in Chihuahua (Mexico) and Regina (Canada) – assistance from Gothenburg (Sweden).
- The sub-region R86 will have the capitals in San Luis Potosi City (Mexico) and Winnipeg (Canada) – assistance from Yverdon-les-Bains (Switzerland).
- The sub-region R87 will have the capitals in Tulsa (OK, USA) and Veracruz (Mexico) – assistance from Bregenz (Austria).
- The sub-region R88 will have the capitals in Memphis (TN, USA) and San José (Costa Rica) – assistance from Uppsala (Sweden).
- The sub-region R89 will have the capitals in Lima (Peru) and Boston (MA, USA) – assistance from Tampere (Finland).

East of Louvre: Place du Louvre, the north tower (1860, with a bell called "Marie", center) of l'Église Saint-Germain l'Auxerrois (founded around 650, rebuilt many times, with a porch which has a rose window, and a balustrade above which encircles the whole church, from 1439, right), and la Mairie du 1er Arrondissment (1859, left). Inside the church are a 15th-century wooden statue of Saint Germain, and a stone carved statue of Saint-Vincent.

In Region R9: from La Paz (Bolivia) to London (United Kingdom)

- The sub-region R90 will have the capitals in La Paz (Bolivia) and Bangor (Maine, USA) – assistance from Aosta (Italy).
- The sub-region R91 will have the capitals in Caracas (Venezuela) and Road Town (British Virgin Islands) – assistance from Obergoms (Switzerland).
- The sub-region R92 will have the capitals in Buenos Aires (Argentina) and Fort-de-France (Martinique) – assistance from Freudenstadt (Germany).
- The sub-region R93 will have the capitals in Asuncion (Paraguay) and Montevideo (Uruguay) – assistance from Winterthur (Switzerland).
- The sub-region R94 will have the capitals in Cayenne (French Guiana), St. John's (Canada) – assistance from Novara (Italy).
- The sub-region R95 will have the capitals in Rio de Janeiro (Brazil) and Dakar (Senegal) – assistance from Toyama (Japan).
- The sub-region R96 will have the capitals in Freetown (Sierra Leone) and Lisbon (Portugal) – assistance from Kawasaki (Japan).
- The sub-region R97 will have the capitals in Bamako (Mali) and Athlone (Ireland) – assistance from Ulm (Germany).
- The sub-region R98 will have the capitals in Yamoussoukro (Cote d'Ivoire) and Madrid (Spain) – assistance from Okayama (Japan).
- The sub-region R99 will have the capitals in Ouagadougou (Burkina Faso) and London (United Kingdom) - assistance from Vaasa (Finland).

Japan, Kyoto (678, it was the imperial capital of Japan for over 1,000 years): Kyoto Tower Hotel, on Shiokoji Dori, 200 m north of Kyoto Railway Station.

Opportunity 12. Explain the Level 3 Management

Description: The objective of this opportunity is to make people familiar with this Level 3 Management.

Qualifications: People with knowledge and experience in this area.

Starting day: 1 January 2021

Ending day: 4 months after starting

Salary: From $34,000/year

Possibility of promotion or transfer to another job: Yes.

Comments: It is useful to have informed people. The ten L3 friendly managers for the 10 regions will supervise and assist the 10 L2 managers of the 10 sub-regions of each region, for a total of about 770,000,000 people for each region.

For example, the Region R0 will have the first capitals in

Bern (Switzerland) and Libreville (Gabon) – assistance from Oxford (UK).

For better quality and consistency of the Qualifications, we'll have the first two cities from the region R0, and the third city from outside. Actually, being inside the same country Terra, any city, sub-region or region can ask for advice or help from anybody.

- The Region R1 will have the first capitals in

Warsaw (Poland) and Pretoria (South Africa) – assistance from Miami (FL, USA).

- The Region R2 will have the first capitals in

Moscow (Russia) and Cairo (Egypt) – assistance from Grenoble (France).

- The Region R3 will have the first capitals in

Astana (Kazakhstan) and Karachi (Pakistan), – assistance from Montpellier (France).

Tokyo, the Skytree (2011, 634 m, a broadcasting, restaurant, and observation tower located in Sumida, north of Asakusa Dori).

- The Region R4 will have the first capitals in

New Delhi (India) and Novosibirsk (Russia) - assistance from Magdeburg (Germany).

- The Region R5 will have the first capitals in

Krasnoyarsk (Russia) and Urumqi (China) - assistance from Avignon (France).

- The Region R6 will have the first capitals in

Jakarta (Indonesia) and Beijing (China) - assistance from Neuchâtel (Switzerland).

- The Region R7 will have the first capitals in

Tokyo (Japan) and Sydney (Australia) - assistance from Malmö (Sweden).

- The Region R8 will have the first capitals in

Washington (USA) and Mexico City (Mexico) - assistance from Bellinzona (Switzerland).

- The Region R9 will have the first capitals in

Halifax (Canada) and Brasilia (Brazil) - assistance from Biel (Switzerland).

USA, Chicago (1833, 2.7 M): Whitehall Hotel (1927, red, right) on E. Delaware Pl., Fourth Presbyterian Church (left down, 1871).

Opportunity 13. Explain the Level 4 Management

Description: The objective of this opportunity is to make people familiar with this Level 4 Management.

Qualifications: People with knowledge and experience in this area.

Starting day: 1 January 2021

Ending day: 4 months after starting

Salary: From $35,000/year

Possibility of promotion or transfer to another job: Yes.

Comments: It is really important to know well to top Management. The level 4 Qualifications are the very friendly 10 Advisers of the world which will supervise and assist the 10 L3 managers of the 10 regions of the Earth, for a total of about 7,700,000,000 people – all the people on Earth, citizens of Peaceful Terra.

Opportunity 14. Work on locations for the 10 Advisors

Description: The objective of this opportunity is to transform many cities by having advisors located there.

Qualifications: People with knowledge and experience in this area.

Starting day: 1 January 2021

Ending day: continuous

Salary: From $34,000/year

Possibility of promotion or transfer to another job: Yes.

Comments: It is an easy and simple opportunity, but important. The 10 Advisors will be located each in one the ten Regions R0, R1,…, R9. For example, in the beginning, for the first month (then changing every month), the ten Advisers of the world will be located:

- in R0: Barcelona (Spain)
- in R1: Benghazi (Libya)
- in R2: Addis Ababa (Ethiopia)
- in R3: Hyderabad (Pakistan)
- in R4: Bhopal (India)
- in R5: Mandalay (Myanmar)
- in R6: Nanchong (China)
- in R7: Khabarovsk (Russia)
- in R8: Houston (USA)
- in R9: Recife (Brazil)

These ten L4 Advisers will be in permanent contact with each other, and with the L3 Advisers, for the best Management of the world.

The ten L4 Advisers will move each month from a first capital of a region to the second capital of another region, at random (or based on urgency, if an emergency occurred). This mobility is essential for having a long period of tranquility and harmony.

The Advisors will be located in the current government buildings, and the excess government buildings and properties will be sold, in order to increase the budget, and to reduce the expenses.

UK, Cambridge, from the entrance to King’s College (1441), looking northwest to the Chapel (the south façade (center left), and the east façade (right)).

Opportunity 15. Maintain technical equipment for the 10 Advisors

Description: The objective of this opportunity is to have good equipment for the top 10 Advisers (and all the others), who will collaborate via e-mail, telephone, videoconferences, mail, or face to face, when needed, to produce practical results for all people, very fast.

Qualifications: People with knowledge and experience in this area.

Starting day: 1 January 2021

Ending day: continuous

Salary: From $36,000/year

Possibility of promotion or transfer to another job: Yes.

Comments: It is essential to have advanced systems for the top Management. The ten L4 Advisers will work by consensus only. It is expected that the 10 Advisors are talented enough to be able to negotiate fast any disagreements between them, and quickly arrive at the best common decision, for the benefit of all people.

Opportunity 16. Working on elections for the 10 Advisors

Description: The objective of this opportunity is to have quiet and civilized elections for the top Managers.

Qualifications: People with knowledge and experience in this area.

Starting day: 1 January 2021

Ending day: continuous

Salary: From $35,000/year

Possibility of promotion or transfer to another job: Yes.

Comments: It is a high priority to have good, calm and friendly elections.

The ten L4 Advisers will be elected from the 10 regions, and each of them will be the First Adviser (***First among equals*** – from Latin: Primus inter pares) for one month, by rotation.

The First Adviser only coordinates the work of the other 9 Advisors for one month.

Opportunity 17. Handle reports from the 10 Advisors

Description: The objective of this opportunity is to keep people informed about the activities of the top 10 Advisors.

Qualifications: People with knowledge and experience in this area.

Starting day: 1 June 2021

Ending day: continuous

Salary: From $37,600/year

Possibility of promotion or transfer to another job: Yes.

Comments: It is imperative to correctly inform people by using a Monthly World Report.

The First Adviser, on the last day of each month, will present in writing for the world (no more than 5 standard pages) a clear and precise Monthly World Report, with a list of finished and unfinished tasks.

The other 9 Advisers will add their comments to the Monthly World Report (no more than half a page each - total report less than 9.5 pages).

In order to better know the world government, to help it, and, especially, to improve it, all able people of the world will work as volunteers at least one day per year in each of the seven departments.

After each Monthly World Report, a public opinion survey about the report should be taken, and presented to all Advisors.

All these activities need people to assist with the practical details.

Opportunity 18. Preserving all Advisors' decisions

Description: The objective of this opportunity is to record all activities of the Advisors, and others from the small World Government, to be available to the people on a website.

Qualifications: People with knowledge and experience in this area.

Starting day: 1 July 2020

Ending day: continuous

Salary: From 35,700/year

Possibility of promotion or transfer to another job: Yes.

Comments: The decisions must be ready for use by all people. The top 10 Advisers will manage Police and all other Departments. All the activities of all Advisors will be recorded in computers and videos, and on paper, for people to be able to see what they are doing. All Advisors are free to speak about their administrative work, with modesty.

Technical and administrative assistance is needed.

Opportunity 19. Forget war mentality

Description: The objective of this opportunity is simply to eliminate the war mentality, in order to help all the people on Earth to live better, peacefully, free, healthy, and prosperous.

Qualifications: People with knowledge and experience in this area.

Starting day: 1 January 2021

Ending day: continuous

Salary: From $28,000/year

Possibility of promotion or transfer to another job: Yes.

Comments: It is a very important effort, useful for everybody. Advisors (and all the others) cannot declare war, reprisals or capture land or water. Advisors (and all the others) cannot raise and support armies, navy, or any military forces.

Teachers and many others need to work really hard to eliminate the war mentality, and to transform it in a happy peace mentality. All people need peace, not war.

Opportunity 20. Work for the 5 assistants

Description: The objective of this opportunity is to prepare the 5 assistants for all managers.

Qualifications: People with knowledge and experience in this area.

Starting day: 1 January 2021

Ending day: continuous

Salary: $62,000/year

Possibility of promotion or transfer to another job: Yes.

Comments: It is a sine qua non requirement to have highly qualified professional to help the government to deliver good services to the population. Each Advisor, and each manager at all levels, will have 5 immediate assistants:
1) a mathematician for finance and all other calculations,
2) a medical doctor for keeping everybody healthy, calm, polite, friendly and optimist,
3) a CEO for good management,
4) an engineer for all practical projects, and
5) a teacher for education, training and related areas.

The five assistants play a key role, because they are highly qualified professionals, who actually will carry on the practical management of the world.

The five assistants' integrity, professionalism and friendliness will significantly improve the quality of the world and local governments.

The five assistants are really the experts. They will assist the Advisors and all levels of management, in order to have an efficient, correct and professional working of the world government at all levels.

All spending proposals from Advisers must be approved by their 5 assistants (doctors, mathematicians, CEOs, engineers and teachers), and must have an already existing funding in the budget.

Obviously, much technical, scientific and advanced managerial help is needed for these assistants.

USA, Boston, 3 Dec 2009, from Avenue Louis Pasteur (1822-1895, French microbiologist), Boston Public Latin School (1635, Schola Latina Bostoniensis, the oldest and the first public exam school in the U.S.).

Opportunity 21. Organizing elections for the Honorific World Observer

Description: The objective of this opportunity is to have quiet and civilized elections for this very special top Management.

Qualifications: People with knowledge and experience in this area.

Starting day: 1 June 2021

Ending day: 2 weeks after election – periodic job, every 3 years

Salary: From $26,000/year

Possibility of promotion or transfer to another job: Yes.

Comments: Serious attention must be given to this process, because of its special importance. An Honorific World Observer will be quietly elected by direct vote – starting, for example, 1st September 2022 - for only one 3 years term, with the main duty to observe that the top 10 Advisers efficiently perform their duties, and keep their words – if they don't, they will be changed. For managers and for everybody else, keeping their word is a serious and strict requirement.

The Honorific World Observer has this responsibility for the top 10 Advisors, but all people will pay attention to this. Words must become again important and respected.

Opportunity 22. Maintenance of the World Government

Description: The objective of this opportunity is to help with the logistics for the World Government in order to work better.

Qualifications: People with knowledge and experience in this area.

Starting day: 1 January 2021

Ending day: continuous

Salary: From $27,000/year

Possibility of promotion or transfer to another job: Yes.

Comments: The World Government needs to be very efficient and economic – all people want this plus peace, freedom, good health, harmony and prosperity.

The World Government will have only 7 Departments, and there are some other important details:

All the employees of the World Government are temporary, and must reapply for their positions every year.

There is no need for unions.

The World Government will be limited to:

1) the Office of the Honorific Observer (less than 10 employees),
2) the Office of the top ten Advisors (less than 100 employees), and
3) 7 small departments.

Good maintenance for the World Government is a high priority activity.

Opportunity 23. Assist the 7 World Government Departments

Description: The objective of this opportunity is to provide specific maintenance work for the World Government Departments.

Qualifications: People with knowledge and experience in this area.

Starting day: 1 January 2021

Ending day: continuous

Salary: From $36,000/year

Possibility of promotion or transfer to another job: Yes.

Comments: It is a matter of common sense – the World Government needs good maintenance and improvements, in order to have for all people peace, freedom, good health, harmony and prosperity.

The World Government will have these 7 small departments:

- Tax Department

- Collects taxes of 15% of the income of people and revenue of companies.

- The Manager of the Tax Department is appointed for a three-year term by the World 10 Advisers.

- The number of employees must be under 50,000, with excellent computers, and advanced software.

On Gagarin (First Man in Space) Terrace, on the southwest part of the South Building (1899) of the Royal Observatory Greenwich (1676), looking northeast to the south part of the west side (right), the west part of the south side (left), and to the statue of Yuri Gagarin (1934-1968, Russian cosmonaut, the first man to journey into space, with Vostok spacecraft, which completed an orbit (1h 48') of the Earth on 12 April 1961. Resting place: Kremlin Wall Necropolis).

- Treasury

Treasury will control all the financial issues, including:
- antitrust
- fiscal service
- financial cooperation
- financing bank
- world reserve system
- world budget using only revenue, no borrowing, and spending only on strict necessary needs
– all the budgets, at all levels, will have a 2% surplus, which will be returned to the taxpayers
- register of all government papers and activities
- archives and records
- assist all people to have savings accounts for old age (the old age will be starting around 70), and 10% of their income should automatically go to their savings accounts. For those unable to work, their doctors and mathematicians will decide case by case.
- bankruptcies, in general, will be discouraged, and when strict necessary, will be analyzed and solved, case by case, by the doctors, mathematicians and CEOs who worked with the people who asked the bankruptcy.
- encourage all families to assist their parents, grandparents, and great-grandparents.
- housing finance
- housing for all people
- no homelessness
- consumer financial protection
- pensions
- privacy
- current social security until replaced by personal savings
- personnel Qualifications
- general services for the world government
- each the 10 regions will receive 2.5% of the world taxes - at least 30% of the money will be sent to villages and cities.
- each of the 100 sub-regions will receive 0.25% of the world taxes. At least 40% of the money will be sent to villages and cities.

- The World Central Bank will include all current central banks – starting, for example, on May 1st, 2023.
- The Special Credit Card (SCC) will be issued by the World Central Bank.
- Advisors will create a new world currency, named, for example, "coin", and all the other currencies will be exchanged for coins. The World Central Bank will implement the details.
- The counterfeiting and all other bad things, which some sick people do, will be medically treated (in specialized medical institutions when necessary), and those who did bad things will pay all the expenses, and will reimburse the victims. Victims will always be very protected, and helped to recover the losses from the attackers.

UK, London, from Newington Butts, in front of the west entrance to the Elephant and Castle Shopping Centre, a small statue Elephant and Castle, and a tall building (left back) with 3 horizontal holes on top.

- People Assistance Department

It will assist people in general, including:
- parent assistance
- dispute resolution
- in very simple disputes or culpa levis (ordinary negligence, like late payments, etc.), one single assistant will decide within minutes, and all people will go back to work
- census every 5 years
- election assistance every 20 months
- special credit cards
- people protection against abuses from anybody
- completely eliminate corruption, organized crime and drug trafficking
- all people in the world will remain in their places, and the improvements will come to them. Those who want to move to other places, will need first a special invitation from at least 10 people (not family related) where they want to move.
- all the Tribunals and related areas will be transformed in people assistance services, based on friendliness, collaboration and goodwill.
- It is well understood that no excessive bail will be required, no excessive fines imposed, no cruel and unusual punishments applied, but, at the same time, it is well understood that a person who did a bad thing will receive the necessary corrective medical treatment, and will reimburse all people who suffered damages, and the medical treatment. The victims will always receive special attention.
- Nobility (King, Prince, etc.) could continue to exist in some places, but they should not interfere with activities of the Advisors, and actually should help them.
- food safety
- trash & recycling
- free commerce
- jobs assistance
- postal service
- labor safety and harmonious relations
- land, water

- volunteers
- fitness, sport, tourism
- 10 world holidays: the normal 4 Earth events (2 solstices (around 21 June, around 21 December), and 2 equinoxes (around 21 March, around 21 September), Mother's Day on 1st May, Father's Day on 6 August, Children's Day on 6 November, Grandparents' Day on 6 February, and 2 optional days (like Thanksgiving or a Religious Day (Christmas), and New Year).

France, Paris, mannequins representing Gustave Eiffel (right, 57 years old) talking in 1889 to Thomas Edison (left, 42 years old) in Eiffel's apartment in Tour Eiffel (1889, 324 m).

- Medical Department

It will manage all medical and healthcare related areas, including:
- human services
- conflict resolution
- families, children, elderly
- medicine approval
- disease control and prevention
- medical doctors and assistants will make regular home visits, at least once a year, to all people, to keep them healthy, and to prevent illnesses.
- medical research: cancer, heart, lung, blood, arthritis, surgical robotics, connected computers for healthcare, etc.
- healthy homes, streets, stores, working places, etc.
- healthy aging
- all misunderstandings, disagreements or conflicts of any nature will be treated by medical personnel (with police help when strict necessary), until all is back to normal.
- no prisons are necessary, only specialized medical institutions (in simple cases, the places where the treated people live can be used, with the necessary limitations and surveillance)
- If a person X is considered that did a bad thing, X will have, within 3 days, a discussion with one or more doctors and other assistants, and will be informed of the nature and cause of the bad thing; including witnesses against and for him. Then a decision will be taken within other 3 days, by a group of doctors and other assistants. Victims of bad people will always have priority to discuss their problems with one or more doctors and other assistants, and quick decisions will be taken within 3 days, by a group of doctors and other assistants. Protection of victims has always priority.
- in order to better know the world government, to help it, and, especially, to improve it, all able people of the world will work as volunteers at least one day per year in the local facility of this department, which will have a special office for managing this volunteer work.

– all people will have government medical insurance, and they can also have private medical insurance
– there will be doctors working for the government 100%, or only part-time, or having only private practice, all with reasonable salaries and fees.
– there will be government pharmaceutical institutions and private pharmaceutical companies, offering reasonable priced medicines, without advertising to the general public.

Japan: the north side of Mt Fuji (3,776 m, 15 km south), from the south of Kawaguchiko (830 m elevation, 100 km south-west of Tokyo), near route 139 Fuji Panorama Line.

- Police

Police will provide assistance for:
- accidents
- disasters
- complete elimination of nuclear, chemical and biological arms, firearms and explosives
- world complete security
- world cooperation
- conflict reduction and resolution
- investigations
- emergency assistance
- training
- delinquency prevention in general, and especially juvenile
- protection of Advisors, important government buildings, etc.
- extended surveillance and reconnaissance to prevent bad events
- fire protection
- volunteers to help police
- police will be present at public meetings, services, shows, etc., in order to protect the public
- public order
- ensuring traffic safety
- completely eliminate corruption, organized crime and drug trafficking
- movement of people based on civilized rules
- assist and protect those who have encountered violence
- World Police and specialists from the former United Nations and Interpol will be ready and very mobile for urgent and special operations, when they are needed.
- Police will be the only department which will have some small arms, in order to stop some very bad people (who are very sick).
- a small manufacturing and maintenance of arms unit will be part of the Police Department, under strict control.
- Police will work with medical personnel, mathematicians, CEOs, engineers, teachers and others, to make sure that all the people on the Planet are in good mental health, in order to prevent bad situations. This is also a major responsibility of all Advisors.

- prevention of bad events
- The Advisors will allocate the necessary budget for Police, and Police will assist people in need.

USA, UC Berkeley (1868), from Campanile (1914, 94 m) looking southwest: Bancroft Library (right down), Doe Memorial Library (next up), Herbarium and Museum of Vertebrate Zoology (center), School of Information (left down), English Dep. (next up), College of Letters & Science, German Dep. (center left), Golden Gate Bridge, San Francisco and the Pacific Ocean (up back).

- Education Department

- Over 2 billions of children in the world will get a solid peace-oriented education, to give a solid peace-oriented foundation for a good, free, peaceful and prosperous life.
- Education is very important – teachers will work with parents and grandparents, to educate the children to leave healthy in a sustainable peace, liberty and prosperity.
- Discipline must be strict, and those who do not behave properly, will get medical assistance.
- The world will have 4 school levels (SLs) of education:

SL1 – Kindergarten – 2 years: age 5 and 6
SL2 – Primary School – 4 years: age 7, 8, 9 and 10
SL3 – Secondary School – 3 years: age 11, 12 and 13
SL4 – High School or Vocational School – 4 years: age 14, 15, 16 and 17

- A World Library will include the Library of Congress and all the other great libraries – they will remain where they are now, but will be digitally interconnected, and accessible from any place in the world.
- adult education: technical, career
- training for employment
- Qualifications training
- post high school education
- peace education
- world constitution education

Japan, Tokyo (1180), special ward Shinjuku: Tokyo Metropolitan Government Building, 243 m, 48 floors, 1991, with two observation decks on floor 45, at 202 m.

- Science & Technology Department.

It will help in the areas of:
- mathematics
- statistics
- science
- technology
- Algorithmic Governance will be an essential tool for a better and impartial governing of the world, used by the Advisers elected by people. Mathematicians from all countries will work to improve the Algorithmic Governance, to better serve the people.
- cyberspace complete security will be achieved and strictly maintained
- information systems
- computer services
- Internet
- scientific cooperation
- economic development at the world level
- infrastructure improvement and maintenance at the world level
- innovation and improvements in all areas, at the world level
- transportation at the world level
- safety
- security
- aviation
- highway
- cars
- railroads without noise
- maritime administration
- logistics
- strategic planning at the world level
- public works
- fleet maintenance
- standards: weights, measures, etc.
- research at the world level
- risk analysis
- laboratories
- engineering

- communications at the world level
- telecommunications
- networks
- peaceful nuclear energy use at the world level
- safety
- waste
- electrical power
- oceanic analysis at the world level
- atmospheric analysis at the global level
- meteorological service and prognosis at the global level
- world resources analysis
- sustainable use of world resources
- geographical and geological activity
- product safety at the global level
- hazardous material and chemical safety
- government broadcasting (radio, tv, Internet, newspaper, etc.) including news, scientific and technical information
- private broadcasting will continue, but the world government must be able to directly inform the people, without intermediaries
- space exploration and expansion at the world level – very important for the future
- patent and trademark
- intellectual rights
- all government work, which can be done by private companies, will be contracted with the best and reasonably priced private companies. At the same time, the government should always have competitive services for people – from plumbing and electrical help, to mortgage and buying or selling a house.

Opportunity 24. Supervise the elections

Description: The objective of this opportunity is to provide good and impartial administration of all the elections.

Qualifications: People with knowledge and experience in this area.

Starting day: 1 January 2021

Ending day: continuous

Salary: From $27,000/year

Possibility of promotion or transfer to another job: Yes.

Comments: Obviously, calm and friendly elections are needed, and their good administration is essential. Political ad spending is over $6.7 B per election; therefore, people's money is transferred to local TV – not good for people. Elections, with zero spending, will be every 20 months.

The Advisers will be elected every 20 months for one term only. If an Adviser X was elected for a term T1, then the next term T2 will have another Advisor Y. For the next term T3, X can be elected again, but the next term T4 will have a new Adviser, and so on. All levels of Advisers (minimum age 25 years) can be elected, not consecutively, at most 4 times (maximum 80 months = 6 years and 8 months).

Advisers should have exceptional results obtained from their work, and based on these results, plus modesty, moderation, good character, friendliness, sharp mind, wisdom, good morals, and intense desire to help people, they will be elected, without any campaigning, publicity, fundraising, donations, debates, propaganda, political parties, advertising, or similar activities.

There will be use of advanced digital technology, which opens up entirely new opportunities for developing direct elections, and public control of the institutions, improving the transparency of the election procedure, and taking into account the interests and opinions of each voter (over the age of 21, who are not in a special medical institution for bad behavior or for mental health).

UK, London: from the Abingdon St., looking southeast to the west façade of the House of Lords of the Palace of Westminster, with the Old Palace Yard, and the equestrian statue of the King Richard I of England (Coeur de Lion or the Lionheart (1157-1199, King 1189-1199, left)).

Venere (Venus) Italica, 1810, by Antonio Canova (1757 – 1822, aged 65, sculptor from Venezia), a carved Carrara marble sculpture, 1.75 m, commissioned by Napoleon Bonaparte (1769 – 1821, aged 52).

Opportunity 25. Verify the qualifications

Description: The objective of this opportunity is to check the qualifications of those who want to run for elections.

Qualifications: People with knowledge and experience in this area.

Starting day: 1 January 2021

Ending day: continuous

Salary: From $40,000/year

Possibility of promotion or transfer to another job: Yes.

Comments: It is very important to have well qualified elected managers. The Election Commission of 110 representatives from the 10 regions and from the 100 sub-regions, elected separately for 5 years, will have to examine the qualifications of all the candidates for Advisers, and for other senior management positions. Unqualified candidates will be asked to improve their qualifications, and then to try again later.

It is important to refresh the management, and to bring new people to help the big family of 7.7 B people. The older generations, who performed well, will be retained in important roles, because experience and maturity count very much. At least two months before the retirement, they will kindly be asked to transfer their expertise to the younger generation. Even after retirement, they will occasionally be invited to share their expertise.

In every election, with every winner, will be other two for number 2 and number 3. The number 2 and number 3 for each management position will be used when number 1 is not available (vacation, sick, etc.). They will constantly work for number 1, helping to solve urgent problems for the people.

Good elections are essential for the future.

There has been a tendency to make elections conflict generating events, with lots of propaganda, false information, heavy donations, unpolite confrontations, bully fundraising, hostile political parties and organizations, unlimited power ambitions, etc.

This will be completely changed into clean, friendly elections, in which people choose between leaders with outstanding results, plus talent to lead people to peace and freedom, modesty, moderation, good character, friendliness, sharp mind, wisdom, good morals, and intense desire to help people – no campaigning, no publicity, no fundraising, no donations, no debates, no propaganda, no political parties, no advertising or similar activities.

The Election Commission, after examining many good candidates, will invite the best to participate in very friendly elections.

UK, London's only planetarium bronze cone (the largest in the world, 250 welded plates). The cone is sliced at angle parallel to celestial equator, the line on the slice is north (left, perpendicular) south (up) is parallel to 0 meridian, angle of the southern side (right) is equal to the latitude of Royal Observatory Greenwich 51° 22' 44" N.

Opportunity 26. Referendum assistance

Description: The objective of this opportunity is to administer all referenda.

Qualifications: People with knowledge and experience in this area.

Starting day: 1 February 2021

Ending day: continuous

Salary: From $27,000/year

Possibility of promotion or transfer to another job: Yes.

Comments: Referendum is a necessity for good government. An electronic world referendum will be organized every three months. The main questions will be:
1. Are you satisfied with the Government?
2. What Government work is good?
3. What Government work is not good?
4: Suggestions for improvement:

Within two months after each referendum, the Government will respond to the people. Based on the suggestions received, new pro-people rules will be replacing some old rules.

USA Chicago (1833): Elysées Condominiums (left, 1972, 56 floors, 161 m), Old Water Tower (left down, 1869, 47 m), 900 North Michigan (center right, 1989, 66 fl, 265 m), One Magnificent Mile (right, 1983, 57 fl, 205 m).

The upper part of the western façade of Cathédrale Notre Dame de Paris (1163 – 1345, 90 m), on the south-eastern part of the Île de la Cité, which is considered the center of Paris, in the fourth arrondissement. The organ has 7,374 pipes, with about 900 classified as historical. It has 110 real stops, five 56-key manuals and a 32-key pedalboard; it is now fully computerized. The Towers at Notre-Dame contain five church bells. The great bourdon bell, Emmanuel, from 1681, 13 t, is located in the South Tower (right).

Opportunity 27. Complete disarmament verification

Description: The objective of this opportunity is to carefully monitor the complete disarmament on the Planet.

Qualifications: Specialized police departments, scientists, and other specialists in this area.

Starting day: 1 January 2021

Ending day: continuous

Salary: From $60,000/year

Possibility of promotion or transfer to another job: Yes.

Comments: It is a matter of common sense – all people want complete disarmament, peace, freedom, good health, harmony and prosperity.

There will be no arms at all:

Arms will not exist anymore, and only the police will have some small arms. Those who want arms for hunting or sport, will borrow them from police stations, with proper documents, rules and payments.

All military units will become strong civilian organizations, working to improve the quality of life for everybody.

A continuous verification and monitoring will be implemented, the make sure that the world finally achieved complete disarmament.

With so many arms now in private hands, it will take a strong effort to collect and destroy all the arms, but it will be done.

Opportunity 28. Census assistance

Description: The objective of this opportunity is administering the census every 5 years.

Qualifications: People with knowledge and experience in this area.

Starting day: 1 October 2023

Ending day: 31 December 2023

Salary: From $22,000/year every 5 years

Possibility of promotion or transfer to another job: Yes.

Comments: Census is necessary to better assist the people. It is also useful for delimitations, special cards, etc. A census will take place every 5 years – starting, for example, on October 1st, 2023 - and all people will receive a special credit card (SCC), with their photo and other personal data. The delimitations between regions, and between sub-regions, will be adjusted by the census.

Opportunity 29. Special Credit Cards assistance

Description: The objective of this opportunity is to help with the administration of the special credit cards for all people.

Qualifications: People with knowledge and experience in this area.

Starting day: 1 January 2021

Ending day: continuous

Salary: From $26,000/year

Possibility of promotion or transfer to another job: Yes.

Comments: It is a matter of common sense – all people need these cards for many things. The special credit card (SCC) will be used to buy everything, to identify for voting (no bureaucratic registration for voting – all people are automatically registered voters), for census, for travel, for medical assistance, etc.

The current private credit cards will continue to work as usual.

The changes of the delimitations between regions, and also sub-regions, will be inputted on these cards, and no other work is needed.

Opportunity 30. Help for virus control and elimination

Description: The objective of this opportunity is a major medical effort for virus control and elimination.

Qualifications: Medical specialists, and people with knowledge and experience in this area.

Starting day: 1 January 2021

Ending day: continuous

Salary: From $49,000/year

Possibility of promotion or transfer to another job: Yes.

Comments: It is a matter of common sense – all people want good health, peace, freedom, harmony and prosperity. People are something sacred for people. The enemies of the people on Earth are not other people, but viruses, microbes, bad bacteria and hundreds of deadly illnesses – all people on Earth will work together against these real enemies for all of us.

Italy, Naples (Napoli, 1500 BC, one of the oldest continuously inhabited cities in the world. The city was refunded as Neápolis around 550 BC, and became a sine qua non of Magna Graecia), the FVNICOLARE building near downtown. The Funicolare Centrale (Central Funicular) is a funicular railway, which is the main part of the metro system for the city of Naples (1928, 1.2 km).

Opportunity 31. Working for Non-violence implementation

Description: The objective of this opportunity is simply to eliminate all forms of violence.

Qualifications: People with knowledge and experience in this area.

Starting day: 1 January 2021

Ending day: continuous

Salary: From $33,000/year

Possibility of promotion or transfer to another job: Yes.

Comments: It is a matter of common sense – all people want non-violence, peace, freedom, good health, harmony and prosperity. Non-violence is directly related to medical assistance. Non-violence is a strict requirement for all activities on Earth. The first rule for everybody on Earth comes from the Hippocratic Oath: Primum non nocere - first do not harm.

Plenty of jobs are in this area.

Opportunity 32. Working to help doctors

Description: The objective of this opportunity is simply to improve people's heath by having regular doctors' home visits.

Qualifications: People with knowledge and experience in this area.

Starting day: 1 January 2021

Ending day: continuous

Salary: From $39,000/year

Possibility of promotion or transfer to another job: Yes.

Comments: It is a matter of common sense – all people want good health, peace, freedom, harmony and prosperity. Home visits will be a real joy! Medical doctors and assistants will make regular home visits to all people, to keep them healthy, and to prevent illnesses.

There are many jobs in this area.

Japan, the entrance to a building with a teaching auditorium, 100 m west from the north-east entrance of the Inzai campus of Tokyo Denki University (a private university founded in 1907, and chartered as a university in 1949), 35 km north-east of Tokyo Imperial Palace, 24 km west of Narita International Airport.

Opportunity 33. Working for truth promotion

Description: The objective of this opportunity is simply to return to the truth.

Qualifications: People with knowledge and experience in this area.

Starting day: 1 January 2021

Ending day: continuous

Salary: $36,000/year

Possibility of promotion or transfer to another job: Yes.

Comments: Truth is needed everywhere, and many people are needed to help. Truth and collaboration are basic elements. People need only truth in order to create a long term peaceful and harmonious society. If someone lies – medical treatment will follow.

The Institut de France (1795, initially in Louvre, moved in 1805 by Napoléon in this baroque building finished in 1684, for Collège des Quatre-Nations) is a revered French cultural society which includes five académies, the most famous being Académie française (1635) and. Académie des sciences (Academy of Sciences), founded in 1666. The Institute, located on Quai de Conti, manages about 1,000 foundations, as well as museums and châteaux. Its Mazarine Library is France's oldest public library.

Opportunity 34. Working for freedom implementation

Description: The objective of this opportunity is simply to have freedom for everybody.

Qualifications: People with knowledge and experience in this area.

Starting day: 1 January 2021

Ending day: continuous

Salary: From $37,000/year

Possibility of promotion or transfer to another job: Yes.

Comments: Freedom is a fundamental requirement on Earth. It is well understood that this freedom refers to doing good things in a civilized manner, not for war, for violence or similar bad things, which are against the wellbeing of the people. Freedom goes hand in hand with responsibility. People can assemble peacefully only.

Many people will have to diligently work on this issue, and it will be a great success.

Opportunity 35. Working for economy improvement

Description: The objective of this opportunity is simply to have a better economy for all.

Qualifications: People with knowledge and experience in this area.

Starting day: 1 January 2021

Ending day: continuous

Salary: From $28,000/year

Possibility of promotion or transfer to another job: Yes.

Comments: The free-market economy is not perfect, but it will be improved. All people will have the option to choose between friendly private services, and friendly government services. Independent assistants and monitors will make sure that there are no abuses. Sine qua non requirements for happiness are morality and free market.

There are jobs for everybody in this area.

Opportunity 36. Working for religion collaboration

Description: The objective of this opportunity is to encourage collaboration between different religions, for the benefit of all people.

Qualifications: People with knowledge and experience in this area.

Starting day: 1 January 2021

Ending day: continuous

Salary: $40,000/year

Possibility of promotion or transfer to another job: Yes.

Comments: It is a matter of common sense – all people want peace, freedom, good health, harmony and prosperity. Competent people will work with great attention in order to find and explain the many common points in all religions – peace, family, love, non-violence, helping each other, etc.

Opportunity 37. Working for government improvement

Description: The objective of this opportunity is simply to make the World Government better.

Qualifications: People with knowledge and experience in this area.

Starting day: 1 January 2021

Ending day: continuous

Salary: $34,000/year

Possibility of promotion or transfer to another job: Yes.

Comments: It is a matter of common sense – all people want better government. People of course can petition the small Word Government, and can change it anytime, if it does not perform as expected.

A great number of jobs will be in this area.

Opportunity 38. Working for balanced budget

Description: The objective of this opportunity is simply to balance the budget, like every good family does.

Qualifications: People with knowledge and experience in this area.

Starting day: 1 January 2021

Ending day: continuous

Salary: From $38,000/year

Possibility of promotion or transfer to another job: Yes.

Comments: All budgets will have surplus of 2% - there will be a strict application of the Latin aphorism: "Sumptus censum ne superset" (Let not your spending exceed your income).

Many will have good jobs in this area.

Opportunity 39. Working for errors elimination

Description: The objective of this opportunity is simply to eliminate the many thousands of errors, which accumulated over the years.

Qualifications: People with knowledge and experience in this area.

Starting day: 1 January 2021

Ending day: continuous

Salary: From $35,000/year

Possibility of promotion or transfer to another job: Yes.

Comments: It is a burning issue - correcting errors is a permanent duty for everybody - Darwin (circa 140 years ago) said "To kill an error is as good a service as, and sometimes even better than, the establishing of a new truth or fact."

Yes, plenty of jobs will be in this area.

Opportunity 40. Working to promote kindness

Description: The objective of this opportunity is simply to always have kindness for everybody.

Qualifications: Teachers, and people with knowledge and experience in this area.

Starting day: 1 January 2021

Ending day: continuous

Salary: From $30,000/year

Possibility of promotion or transfer to another job: Yes.

Comments: Kindness is a necessity – it is a requirement for everybody. Seneca (circa 1,960 years ago) said "Wherever there is a human being, there is an opportunity for a kindness." This is a fundamental idea which must be constantly applied.

Therefore, kind people will have many jobs in this area.

Italy, Rome (753 BC), Piazza di Monte Citorio, Camera dei Deputati (back), from Via della Guglia the view of the Obelisk of Montecitorio (or Solare, 21.79 m, 33.97 m with base and globe, moved here in 1789): an ancient Egyptian red granite obelisk of Psammetichus II (595-589 BC) from Heliopolis, brought to Rome with the Flaminian obelisk in 10 BC by the Roman Emperor Augustus (63 BC – 14 AD) to be used as the gnomon (the part of a sundial that casts the shadow) of the Solarium (or Horologium) Augusti (10 BC, functioned as a giant Solar clock, built by the mathematician Facondius Novus (circa 50 BC – 15 AD).

Opportunity 41. Working for Government mobility

Description: The objective of this opportunity is to have a very mobile government, which goes to people, not vice-versa.

Qualifications: People with knowledge and experience in this area.

Starting day: 1 January 2021

Ending day: continuous

Salary: From $38,000/year

Possibility of promotion or transfer to another job: Yes.

Comments: The more mobility the government has, the better people will be served. All levels of government will be highly mobile - changing of the capitals for the 10 regions, and for the 100 sub-regions, etc. It is necessary to move the government close to the people, to be able to quickly solve the local problems.

Obviously, many jobs will be around.

Opportunity 42. Work to have friendly world police

Description: The objective of this opportunity is to have a very friendly world police.

Qualifications: People with knowledge and experience in this area.

Starting day: 1 January 2021

Ending day: continuous

Salary: From $38,000/year

Possibility of promotion or transfer to another job: Yes.

Comments: It is a matter of common sense – all people want peace, freedom, good health, harmony, prosperity, and friendly police to help them when necessary. Police will help people everywhere. The United Nations will change in 2-3 years (for example, by 2024) into World Police and Assistance Organization (WPAO), to help local police in case of big natural disasters or big accidents, and will report to the top 10 Advisers. The police will be located in all capitals, and help the locals. When an emergency appears, they will quickly move to solve the emergency.

The police powers will be limited, and they will know and be friend with all the people in their jurisdiction – this is the key element of a civilized and peaceful Earth.

Police will be people's friends everywhere, and they will always help people.

Prevention of bad events is the main objective of everybody. If a bad event occurs, the police and their assistants will eliminate the consequences, reestablish the normal situation, and determine why the bad event occurred, in order to improve their activity, and prevent such bad events in the future.

In order to prevent bad things, the police, doctors and their assistants will be in permanent contact with all the people, by visiting them, phone calls, e-mails, tele-videos, and mail, to keep everybody calm and happy.

Many jobs will be available for this important objective.

Italy, Rome (753 BC), the goddess Diana (1590, the symbol of Chastity, by Domenico Fontana) is one (in the north) of the Quatro Fontane (the four Fountains: River Tiber, River Arno, goddess Juno) at the intersection of Via del Quirinale and Via delle Quatro Fontane.

Opportunity 43. Working for non-stop Government

Description: The objective of this opportunity is to assist the government to work continuously.

Qualifications: People with knowledge and experience in this area.

Starting day: 1 January 2021

Ending day: continuous

Salary: From $25,000/year

Possibility of promotion or transfer to another job: Yes.

Comments: It is only normal to have always someone in the government to help. About 66% of the Government will always be working somewhere on the Earth - if people need help, they can always call the Government. Non-stop working of all world government departments – especially medical, police, emergency, volunteers – will be carefully organized.

To help this process, many jobs will be around.

Japan, Nikko, (140 km north of Tokyo, with 103 shrines and temples): a stone lantern and tall trees with ornaments, near Betsugu Taki-no-o-jinja Karamon (left, 1740, gate of the Betsugu Taki-no-o-jinja Honden (1619), part of the 23 structures of the Futarasan Shrine (1619)).

Opportunity 44. Working for respect of privacy

Description: The objective of this opportunity is simply to increase the respect for privacy.

Qualifications: People with knowledge and experience in this area.

Starting day: 1 January 2021

Ending day: continuous

Salary: From $24,000/year

Possibility of promotion or transfer to another job: Yes.

Comments: It is clear that privacy is needed. Privacy of negotiations and discussions are necessary. In order to have serious and constructive discussions and negotiations, they must be private.

Privacy and discipline are necessary for good government work.

The results will be public and preserved, but not the private discussions.

Good jobs will be available.

Opportunity 45. Polite Government

Description: The objective of this opportunity is simply to create a very polite government. Impossible? No! Inevitable? Yes!

Qualifications: People with knowledge and experience in this area.

Starting day: 1 January 2021

Ending day: continuous

Salary: starting at $27,000/year

Possibility of promotion or transfer to another job: Yes.

Comments: All people want polite government, peace, freedom, good health, harmony and prosperity.

It is a strict requirement for the top managements, and for all others, to be highly civilized, polite, courteous, harmonious and efficient.

Who wants to work for the world government must have good manners.

Harmony in the world starts from the harmony and good manners of the people in the world government.

Because all people on Earth want to live in harmony right now, it will be relatively easy to implement this in one good and civilized country. This may include having small, beautiful and commonly agreed fences around properties, because good fences make good neighbors, and also helps with more privacy.

So, plenty of jobs.

Rome (753 BC), Vatican (1929): Piazza di San Pietro (1656 – 1667, Bernini), the south part of the portico of the Basilica Papale di San Pietro (1506 – 1626,), with a private entrance to the Vatican City. A halberdier (left down) of the Pontificia Cohors Helvetica (Pontifical Swiss Guard, from 1506, 135 men), with a halberd.

Opportunity 46. Working for conflict resolution

Description: The objective of this opportunity is to eliminate all types of conflicts on Earth.

Qualifications: People with knowledge and experience in this area.

Starting day: 1 January 2021

Ending day: continuous

Salary: from $24,000/year

Possibility of promotion or transfer to another job: Yes.

Comments: All people want no conflicts, peace, freedom, good health, harmony and prosperity. All conflicts must not only be quickly resolved, but they also must be transformed in friendships. This is very important for long term stability.

The medical personnel and others will work diligently to make sure that disputes are resolved, and then a friendship is developed. Only in this way the situation will become stable. Conflicts will be quickly resolved, and then the corrective medical treatment will include the transformation of hostility and aggressiveness into harmony and friendship.

Dispute resolution is not only Government's obligation, but it will be everybody's duty. There will be professional assistance from medical personnel, police, people assistance specialists, volunteers, religious organizations, and many others, but the bottom line is that everybody must avoid disputes.

Therefore, great jobs for those talented in this area.

Opportunity 47. Common language and alphabet

Description: The objective of this opportunity is simply to establish a common language and alphabet.

Qualifications: Teachers and people with knowledge and experience in this area.

Starting day: 1 January 2021

Ending day: continuous

Salary: from $30,000/year

Possibility of promotion or transfer to another job: Yes.

Comments: It is a matter of common sense – all people want to easily communicate between themselves, to have peace, freedom, good health, harmony and prosperity. As a single big, over 7.7 B, family on Earth, all people must be able to communicate easily with each other. For this reason, a common language and alphabet on Earth are needed. Because English is a de facto common language now, it will be taken as the basis of the world language, let's call it Mundo, which will be taught in all schools, and used in the world government. All the other languages will continue as secondary languages. The same is true for the Latin alphabet, which will be used everywhere, with other alphabets as secondary. The teachers will have a very significant role in implementing this opportunity, and many others will have good jobs helping the teachers.

UK, London, the west front of St. Paul's Cathedral (1697, 158 m by 75 m, height 111 m, 2 towers on this side, Anglican cathedral, the seat of the Bishop of London, on Ludgate Hill, at the highest point of London, Canaletto (1697-1768), in 1746, painted The River Thames with St. Paul's Cathedral on Lord Mayor's Day), Statue of Queen Anne (1665-1714, reign 1702-1714, in 1707 England and Scotland formed Great Britain).

Opportunity 48. Increasing global wealth

Description: The objective of this opportunity is to increase the global wealth.

Qualifications: People with knowledge and experience in this area.

Starting day: 1 January 2021

Ending day: continuous

Salary: From $50,000/year

Possibility of promotion or transfer to another job: Yes.

Comments: Obviously, all the global wealth will be carefully used only for peace, freedom and prosperity for all. The 2018 Global Wealth Report from Credit Suisse shows that the total global wealth has reached $317 trillions (circa $41,000/person), which is encouraging, and all this wealth must be increased and used only for peace. To increase the global wealth, everybody will be encouraged to improve everything, to create, to innovate, to research, to develop, to produce new and better products for all people, etc. It is a major responsibility of the Government to increase the global wealth, and to train those in need, to have better working abilities and opportunities. Plenty of great jobs for innovators, researchers, creators, developers, etc.

France, Paris, The Panthéon (1758 - 1790, 83 m height, mausoleum in the Latin Quarter in Paris, modeled on the Pantheon in Rome), seen from the west end of Rue Soufflot, near Jardin du Luxembourg (1612). This mausoleum, with the motto: *Aux grands hommes, la patrie reconnaissante* ("To the great men, the grateful homeland"), contains the remains of distinguished French citizens (Voltaire, Rousseau, Victor Hugo, etc.). In 1851, physicist Léon Foucault demonstrated the rotation of the earth by his experiment conducted in the Panthéon, by constructing a 67 m Foucault pendulum beneath the central dome.

Opportunity 49. Working on bureaucracy elimination

Description: The objective of this opportunity is to eliminate bureaucracy.

Qualifications: All people interested in the elimination of bureaucracy.

Starting day: 1 January 2021

Ending day: continuous

Salary: Starting at $27,000/year

Possibility of promotion or transfer to another job: Yes.

Comments: The goal is no bureaucracy whatsoever. In a well-organized country, with all people working together in harmony, this can be accomplished in several years.
Constant attention will be focused on avoiding duplication at all levels of the world government – there must be continuous collaboration between all levels, to prevent duplication, and to eliminate it, if it was found.
Numerous jobs for people interested in the elimination of bureaucracy.

Opportunity 50. Working for corruption eradication

Description: The objective of this opportunity is to eradicate corruption.

Qualifications: All people interested in the elimination of corruption.

Starting day: 1 January 2021

Ending day: continuous

Salary: Starting at $28,000.

Possibility of promotion or transfer to another job: Yes.

Comments: Everybody can have a good job to work really hard to completely eliminate corruption, organized crime and drug trafficking. Those involved in such bad activities will receive corrective medical treatment, until they become good working people.

Opportunity 51. Working to encourage savings

Description: The objective of this opportunity is simply to encourage savings.

Qualifications: People who know to balance family budgets, and want to help others.

Starting day: 1 January 2021

Ending day: continuous

Salary: From $30,000/year

Possibility of promotion or transfer to another job: Yes.

Comments: A world reserve system will be created.

Each government department will have some reserves for special situations (natural disasters, big accidents), and the banks will also have good financial reserves.

All people can have a good job to encourage other people to save some money in banks which pay 5% interest.

Opportunity 52. Working for Government efficiency

Description: The objective of this opportunity is to improve government efficiency.

Qualifications: People with knowledge and experience in improving government efficiency.

Starting day: 1 January 2021

Ending day: continuous

Salary: From $40,000/year

Possibility of promotion or transfer to another job: Yes.

Comments: Inspectors will help the Government with the integrity and efficiency issues – always there are ways to improve the work.

Inspectors will give advice regarding integrity and efficiency, and will take corrective actions when necessary.

Plenty of good jobs to improve government efficiency.

Opportunity 53. Family assistance

Description: The objective of this opportunity is simply to assist all families.

Qualifications: People with knowledge and experience in family assistance.

Starting day: 1 January 2021

Ending day: continuous

Salary: From $36,000/year.

Possibility of promotion or transfer to another job: Yes.

Comments: It is a matter of common sense – all people want healthy families with happy children, peace, freedom, good health, harmony and prosperity.

Because all families need assistance from time to time, and the big 7.7 B family on Earth contains billions of small families, all of them will have the assistance they need – this will be the result of one country well organized and managed.

All people can have great jobs to assist families.

Opportunity 54. Abuse purging

Description: The objective of this opportunity is to get rid of abuses, which are quite frequent.

Qualifications: People who have knowledge and experience in finding, analyzing and correcting abuses.

Starting day: 1 January 2021

Ending day: continuous

Salary: From $47,000/year.

Possibility of promotion or transfer to another job: Yes.

Comments: It is a demanding effort, after thousands of years of all kinds of abuses, but the abuses will be gone!

Special attention will be given by Advisors to avoid abuses and wrong interpretations of the rules. All assistants (doctors, mathematicians, CEOs, engineers and teachers) will closely monitor all activities, to avoid abuses and wrong interpretations of the rules.

This requirement of not having abuses is demanding – but this is a general job, not only for Government – it is everybody, as part of the big family, we just don't need abuses.

The abuse, in some places, of confiscating the land by some government bureaucrats will be eliminated – the land belongs to the people, not the government.

The abuse, in some places, of having trains, airplanes, and others making unhealthy noises, with the government support, will be eliminated – peoples' health has always priority.

The abuse, in some places, of having to change the clocks twice a year will be eliminated – only the normal local time zones will be used.

If abuses are observed, they will be immediately reported to the Government, and corrected, in general, by the People Assistance

Department, which will have personnel, including medical assistants, to analyze and promptly solve the abuses. The abusers will undergo corrective medical treatment, and will pay significant financial charges.

As we can see, there are plenty of good jobs for this demanding task of eliminating abuses.

Italy, Udine: 3 Nov 2009, Piazza della Liberta, looking east to Porticato di San Giovanni (1533, left), Via Vittorio Veneto (center right back), il Campanile della Chiesa del Duomo (center right up), the column (1539) with San Marco's lion (the symbol of Venezia, right).

Opportunity 55. Working for free commerce

Description: The objective of this opportunity is simply to encourage free commerce.

Qualifications: People with knowledge and experience in commerce.

Starting day: 1 January 2021

Ending day: continuous

Salary: From $25,000/year

Possibility of promotion or transfer to another job: Yes.

Comments: People need intense free commerce.

In one country, with one market, the commerce between the people on Earth will be free of taxes, tariffs, duties, etc. – plenty of jobs for everybody.

Opportunity 56. Working for free and responsible speech and press

Description: The objective of this opportunity is simply to make sure that there is free and responsible speech and press.

Qualifications: People with knowledge and experience in free and responsible speech and press.

Starting day: 1 January 2021

Ending day: continuous

Salary: From $43,000/year.

Possibility of promotion or transfer to another job: Yes.

Comments: People need free and responsible speech and press.

It is expected not to call for war, violence, or similar destructive activities. People want peace, freedom, health, friendship and prosperity.

Good jobs for those qualified for this important opportunity.

France, Paris, Musée du Louvre (1793, in Palais du Louvre (1550)): from Cour Napoléon (between 1862-1867 Napoléon III reunited les Tuileries au Louvre), the right side of the central part of the western façade of Pavillon de l'Horloge or Pavillon Sully (1624 – 1654, under Kings Louis XIII (1601 – 1643, reign 1610 – 1643), and Louis XIV (1638 – 1715, reign 1643 – 1715)), which is on the east side of Cour Napoléon and of the west side of Cour Carrée.

Opportunity 57. Working for government integrity

Description: The objective of this opportunity is simply to improve the government integrity.

Qualifications: People with knowledge and experience in government integrity.

Starting day: 1 January 2021

Ending day: continuous

Salary: From $43,000/year

Possibility of promotion or transfer to another job: Yes.

Comments: A Latin proverb says: “Integrity is the noblest possession”. With this in mind, good jobs will be available for those qualified to work on improving the government integrity.

Opportunity 58. Working for peaceful assemble

Description: The objective of this opportunity is simply to assist in organizing peaceful assembly.

Qualifications: People with knowledge and experience in organizing peaceful assembly and meetings.

Starting day: 1 January 2021.

Ending day: continuous.

Salary: From $38,000/year.

Possibility of promotion or transfer to another job: Yes.

Comments: People want peaceful assembly, when needed.

If some disagree with a decision, they can always inform the government, which will respond in 3 days. The discussion will continue with calm and respect, until everything is clarified.

People can assemble peacefully only, with police for help. It is expected not to call for war, violence, or similar destructive activities. People want peace, freedom, health, friendship and prosperity. If some use violence, they will undergo corrective medical treatment, and will pay significant financial fees.

There will be need for people qualified in organizing peaceful assembly and meetings, therefore good jobs for them.

USA, Boston: 3 Dec 2009, from Harvard Medical School looking northeast to the Avenue Louis Pasteur (1822-1895, French microbiologist),

Switzerland, Geneva, on Quai du Général Guisan (1874-1960), going southeast, Swissotel (center), Jardin Anglais (left), Place des Florentins (right).

Opportunity 59. Helping people to find jobs

Description: The objective of this opportunity is simply to help people to find jobs.

Qualifications: People with knowledge and experience in assisting people to find jobs.

Starting day: 1 January 2021

Ending day: continuous

Salary: From $37,000/year.

Possibility of promotion or transfer to another job: Yes.

Comments: There will always be plenty of jobs at world minimum wage (assisting other people, for example), and the standard situation will be this: more jobs than available people, so people will choose the jobs they like the most.

Good jobs for those qualified in assisting people to find jobs.

Opportunity 60. Working for clean and safe streets

Description: The objective of this opportunity is simply to have clean and safe streets everywhere.

Qualifications: All people interested in clean and safe streets everywhere.

Starting day: 1 January 2021

Ending day: continuous

Salary: From 24,000/year

Possibility of promotion or transfer to another job: Yes.

Comments: People want no unemployment, no homelessness, no begging, no tipping - just all working harmoniously, having good houses, and helping each other. When necessary, corrective medical treatment and significant financial fees will be applied.

Many jobs will be available in this area.

USA, 5 Feb 2016, driving in winter 30 km northwest of Boston, on Lowell Street (5 km east of Lowell), in Andover (1642, population 34,000, named after Andover (circa 955, county of Hampshire, 100 km southwest of London, 60 km south of Oxford, England, population 64,000)). The highly selective Phillips Academy Andover (1778, the oldest incorporated high school in the USA) is a College preparatory high school (grades 9-12, 1122 students).

Opportunity 61. Working for constitution stability

Description: The objective of this opportunity is to help the Constitution stability.

Qualifications: People with knowledge and experience in Constitution stability.

Starting day: 1 January 2021

Ending day: continuous

Salary: From $48,000/year.

Possibility of promotion or transfer to another job: Yes.

Comments: The Constitution of the World can be improved when 66% of the voters agree.

Great jobs are available for those qualified – it is important to have stability, peace and freedom – then changes will take place in a calm and friendly atmosphere.

UK, London, from the Westminster Bridge (1862) looking southwest to the southern part of Palace of Westminster (1016, 1870, right), a tall residential building (center left) near Millbank Millennium Pier, and The Tower (left, condominium complex, on Nine Elms Lane).

Opportunity 62. Working for space exploration

Description: The objective of this opportunity is simply to enhance space exploration.

Qualifications: Experts in space exploration.

Starting day: 1 November 2021

Ending day: continuous

Salary: From $60,000/year

Possibility of promotion or transfer to another job: Yes.

Comments: The purpose for all people on Earth is to be healthy, to live in peace, freedom and harmony, to be prosperous, and to prepare to expand to the Moon, asteroids, Mars, and other places in the Universe, which can support life.

Specialists in this area – like rachet production, Earth observation data, orbital operations, ground station networks, launch services, broadband communications, Moon operations, manufacturing in space – will have great jobs.

Opportunity 63. Robots and automated processes for people

Description: The objective of this opportunity is to have many robots and automated processes for people, to live better.

Qualifications: Experts in robots and automated processes.

Starting day: 1 January 2021

Ending day: continuous

Salary: From $60,000/year.

Possibility of promotion or transfer to another job: Yes.

Comments: It is clear that robots and automated processes for people will help them to live better.

Important immediate objectives for everybody are to reserve time for happiness, use robots and automated processes, work less, and spend more time with your family.

Make civilized behavior and harmony everywhere is an important issue.

Robots help to eliminate stress, and also to help friends and colleagues.

Medical robots can keep everybody relaxed, calm, friendly, patient, and happy.

Experts in this area will have numerous jobs.

Opportunity 64. Working to start a new structure of the world

Description: The objective of this opportunity is to start a new structure of the world.

Qualifications: People with knowledge and experience in starting new structures.

Starting day: 1 January 2021

Ending day: 1 year after starting.

Salary: From $47,000/year.

Possibility of promotion or transfer to another job: Yes.

Comments: To start this new structure of the world, one idea could be this: the first Honorific World Observer (from UN, for example) could invite 10 Presidents form big countries (like USA, China, Russia, UK, India, France, Japan, Germany, Brasil, and Egypt) to be the first 10 Advisors Level 4, starting, for example, on January 1st, 2021, for 10 months, until November 1st, 2021, when the new calm and noiseless elections will take place. The same for the 100 Advisers Level 3, and so on.

It is a little difficult at the beginning, but people will certainly succeed.

Plenty of good jobs in this area.

Opportunity 65. Helping with books

Description: The objective of this opportunity is simply to help people with good books

Qualifications: Teachers, and many others interested in books related to the new World Constitution.

Starting day: 1 January 2021

Ending day: continuous

Salary: From $24,000/year

Possibility of promotion or transfer to another job:

Comments: Good books are always useful, especially when people want to achieve peace, freedom, good health, harmony and prosperity.

For better understanding and easier implementation of the World Constitution, the following books, by Michael M. Dediu, are recommended:

- Our Future is Sustainable Peace and Prosperity – Moving from conflicts to harmony and peace
– Our Future Depends on Good World Educations – Moving from frail education to solid education.
– Friendly, Helpful & Smart World Qualifications - Moving from bureaucracy to responsive world Qualifications
– If You Want Peace, Prepare for Peace! – Moving from preparation for war to preparation for peace
– World with One Country & its Ten Friendly Regions - Moving from 195 disagreeing countries, to 1 country with 10 collaborating regions
– After 10,000 Years of Conflicts, People want 10,000 Years of Harmony - Moving from continuous wars to stable peace

- The Constitution of the World – Moving from many unsustainable constitutions, to just one Constitution of the World
- World Constitution Implementation – Moving from violent changes, to smooth transition to the Constitution of the World
- It is getting truer and truer – we urgently need the World Constitution: Moving from anarchic changes, to balanced transition to the Constitution of the World
- World Constitution with Lovely Comments - Moving from many suboptimal constitutions to the much better Constitution of the World
- World Constitution with Questions & Answers – Moving from many obsolete constitutions to the much better Constitution of the World
- World Projects - Moving from minor projects to great projects for the World
- Dediu Newsletter, Volume 4, Number 12 (48), 6 November 2020 – World Monthly Report

No question that many jobs will be available in this area.

UK, London, from the Shard (2012, 309 m, observatory at 244 m), looking east to the Tower Bridge (1886-1894, combined bascule and suspension turreted bridge over River Thames (flowing from west (left) to east (right)), between London boroughs Tower Hamlets (north – left up) and Southwark (south – right), length 244 m, height 65 m, longest span 82 m, clearance 8 m (closed), 42 m (open)), City Hall (2002, height 45 m, center right round, for the Greater London Authority: Mayor of London and the London Assembly).

Opportunity 66. Work for hurricane prevention

Description: The objective of this opportunity is to prevent hurricanes.

Qualifications: Good engineers, mathematicians, CEOs, and other specialists from the world, as well as talented people interested in advanced work

Starting day: 1 January 2021

Ending day: continuous

Salary: From $44,000/year

Possibility of promotion or transfer to another job: Yes

Comments: Hurricanes can be prevented with some significant engineering techniques – all depends on the good management of this opportunity.

Qualified people will have great jobs, with beautiful results.

Opportunity 67. Working for long term harmony

Description: The objective of this opportunity is to create conditions for long term harmony.

Qualifications: People interested in working in harmony with others.

Starting day: 1 January 2021

Ending day: continuous

Salary: From $17,000/year.

Possibility of promotion or transfer to another job: Yes.

Comments: The objective is to have at least 10,000 years of harmonious living on the happy Earth, therefore numerous jobs will be available for everybody.

Italy, Rome (753 BC, one of the oldest cities in Europe, called Roma Aeterna (The Eternal City) and Caput Mundi (Capital of the World)), from the Pincian Hill looking southwest: Piazza del Popolo (1822), with the Egyptian obelisk (36 m) of Sety I (1290–1279 BC) and Rameses II (1303, 1279–1213 BC) from Heliopolis, brought in 10 BC by Augustus (63 BC-14 AD) for Circus Maximus, in 1589 here. Basilica San Pietro (1506, 132 m, back).

Opportunity 68. Working for the new World Constitution

Description: The objective of this opportunity is simply to promote the new World Constitution.

Qualifications: People interested in a much better life using the new World Constitution

Starting day: 1 January 2021

Ending day: continuous

Salary: $36,000/year.

Possibility of promotion or transfer to another job: Yes.

Comments: It is nice to know that the Constitution of the World is ready to come into force, and to be put into practice, for the benefit of all people on Earth, on 6 March 2020, and it is ready to remain into force, and enjoyed by all people, at least until 6 March 12020.

Like with any new world structure, it is necessary to explain all the benefits, therefore good jobs are waiting for those interested.

Opportunity 69. Working for noise reduction and elimination

Description: The objective of this opportunity is to reduce and eliminate noise by using advanced technology.

Qualifications: Good engineers, and other talented people interested in advanced technology

Starting day: 1 January 2021

Ending day: continuous

Salary: $54,000/year

Possibility of promotion or transfer to another job: Yes.

Comments: There are many advanced technologies, which can significantly reduce or eliminate noise everywhere – all depends on the good management of this opportunity.

Specialists will have numerous jobs waiting for them.

Opportunity 70. Working for zero-injury everywhere

Description: The objective of this opportunity is simply to eliminate injuries everywhere.

Qualifications: Doctors, engineers, mathematicians, and other talented people interested in eliminating injuries.

Starting day: 1 January 2021

Ending day: continuous

Salary: From $56,000/year

Possibility of promotion or transfer to another job: Yes.

Comments: Using advanced technology, the injuries can be avoided everywhere.

It is an ambitious project, but good specialists, with many helpers, will certainly achieve the objective.

Opportunity 71. Working for zero-incident everywhere

Description: The objective of this opportunity is simply to eliminate incidents everywhere.

Qualifications: Police, doctors, teachers, and other talented people interested in eliminating incidents everywhere.

Starting day: 1 January 2021

Ending day: continuous

Salary: From $44,000/year

Possibility of promotion or transfer to another job: Yes.

Comments: Using advanced technology, the incidents can be avoided everywhere.

Again, it is a demanding project, but on a well managed Earth, it will be successful, creating numerous jobs.

Opportunity 72. Working for earthquake forecasting

Description: The objective of this opportunity is to better forecast earthquakes.

Qualifications: Good specialists in earthquakes, mathematicians, engineers, and other talented people interested in earthquake forecasting.

Starting day: 1 January 2021

Ending day: continuous

Salary: $63,000/year

Possibility of promotion or transfer to another job: Yes.

Comments: It is a difficult task, but with more concentrated technological efforts, much better forecasting can be achieved.

Plenty of great jobs for good specialists in this domain.

Opportunity 73. Other ideas for Opportunities

There are many thousands for very important and urgent world opportunities, which will employ millions of people for very useful purposes – here are some examples:

- Flood prevention – it is possible with advanced technology.
- Drought prevention - it is possible with advanced technology.
- Dental assistance – all people will have access to good dental assistance
- Trees maintenance – all trees need maintenance, and it will be done the right way
- Sewer maintenance – all people will have public sewer and it will be properly maintained
- Product quality control – all products will be of good quality, for customers' benefit
- Home services – all home services will be easily available
- Business-customer harmony – it will be achieved
- Mortgages for people – less than 5 pages, no fees, less than 3 days
- Global opportunities for all in agriculture, commerce, construction, etc.
- Human error reduction
- Global goal of reducing road traffic casualties
- Increasing personal responsibility

Many such opportunities are waiting to be implemented, for people's benefit, creating numerous great jobs for everybody.

Italy, Roma (753 BC, one of the oldest occupied cities in Europe, called Roma Aeterna (The Eternal City) and Caput Mundi (Capital of the World)), southeast of Piazza del Popolo (1822, by Giuseppe Valadier, inside the northern gate in the Aurelian Walls, the Porta Flaminia, now called the Porta del Popolo), near Via del Babuino (opened in 1525 as the Via Paolina) and the church Santa Maria in Montesanto (1679, begun by Rainaldi and completed by Bernini and Fontana), the statue of the Goddess of Abundance.

www.ingramcontent.com/pod-product-compliance
Lightning Source LLC
LaVergne TN
LVHW052251100826
845147LV00001B/16

* 9 7 8 1 9 5 0 9 9 9 2 6 2 *